September 11, 2001:

The Day That Changed America

By Jill C. Wheeler

Visit us at
www.abdopub.com

Published by ABDO & Daughters, an imprint of ABDO Publishing Company, 4940 Viking Drive, Suite 622, Edina, Minnesota 55435. Copyright ©2002 by Abdo Consulting Group, Inc. International copyrights reserved in all countries. No part of this book may be reproduced in any form without written permission from the publisher.

Second Edition.
Printed in the United States.

Edited by Paul Joseph
Graphic Design: John Hamilton
Cover Design: Mighty Media
Photos: AP/Photo, FEMA, SpaceImaging.com, Airliners.net
Illustrations: John Hamilton

Library of Congress Cataloging-in-Publication Data

Wheeler, Jill C., 1964-
     September 11, 2001: the day that changed America / Jill C. Wheeler
     p. cm. —(War on terrorism)
     Includes index.
     Summary: Describes the events and immediate aftermath of the September 11, 2001 terrorist attacks on the United States, in which planes were crashed into the Twin Towers buildings in New York City as well as into the Pentagon building near Washington, D.C.
     ISBN 1-57765-656-3
     1. September 11 Terrorist Attacks, 2001—Juvenile literature. 2. Terrorism—New York (State)—New York—Juvenile literature. 3. Terrorism—United States—Juvenile literature. 4. Disasters—New York (State)—New York—Juvenile literature. [1. September 11 Terrorist Attacks, 2001. 2. Terrorism. 3. Disasters.] I. Title: Day that changed America. II. Title. III. Series.

HV6432.W48 2002
973.931—dc 21
                                                                              2001053930

Table of Contents

DAY OF

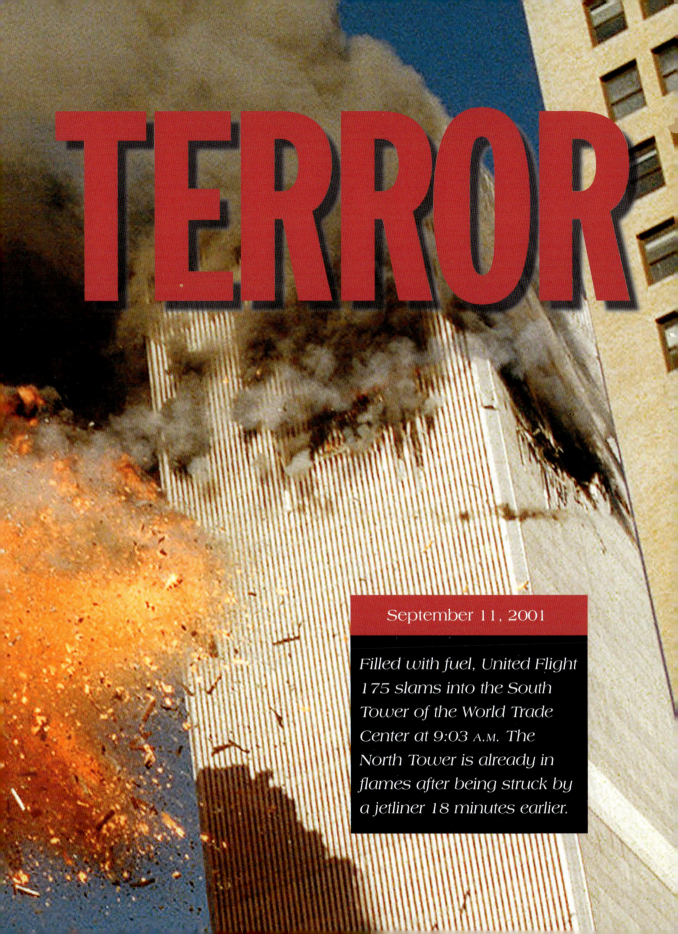

TERROR

September 11, 2001

Filled with fuel, United Flight 175 slams into the South Tower of the World Trade Center at 9:03 A.M. The North Tower is already in flames after being struck by a jetliner 18 minutes earlier.

The Inferno

Fire and smoke billow from the North Tower of New York's World Trade Center.

The Towers Collapse

New Yorkers flee in terror from the collapse of the World Trade Center towers.

Ground Zero

Rescue workers pick through the rubble of the World Trade Center. More than 3,000 innocent people lost their lives in the terrorist attacks.

The Missing

Relatives of people missing in the World Trade Center collapse posted photos of their loved ones outside New York area hospitals.

"Terrorist attacks can shake the foundations of our biggest buildings, but they cannot touch the foundation of America."
President George W. Bush

Mourning In America

TUESDAY, SEPTEMBER 11, 2001, DAWNED CRISP and clear along the United States' eastern seaboard. The warm sunshine spoke of summer. The crisp blue sky held the promise of fall. Thirty-five-year-old Madeline Sweeney might have enjoyed taking the day off to enjoy the perfect weather. Instead she reported for work at Logan International Airport in Boston, Massachusetts. She was a flight attendant for American Airlines. That day, she was scheduled to work on American Flight 11 from Boston to Los Angeles, California.

The flight began much like the thousands of other flights Sweeney had worked in her 12 years as a flight attendant. The Boeing 767 took off from Boston at 7:58 a.m. with 92 passengers and crew on board.

That same morning, Michael Woodward was working as a ground manager at Logan. Less than an hour after Flight 11 took off, he answered his phone and heard Sweeney on the other end. She was calling from the airplane. "This plane has been hijacked," she told him. She went on to say the hijackers had stabbed two flight attendants. She also said it appeared the hijackers had killed a passenger.

15

Alarmed, Woodward asked her where the plane was. "I see water and buildings," Sweeney said. Then she added, "Oh, my God! Oh, my God!" Suddenly, the phone went dead.

Within hours, Woodward and millions of other Americans learned the awful truth about Flight 11. The water Sweeney had seen was New York Harbor. The buildings were in Manhattan. At 8:46 A.M., Flight 11 smashed into the 110-story-tall North Tower of the World Trade Center (WTC). The plane crashed into the tower's north face just above the 90th floor. "Both wings broke right off, then the tail fell off," said a witness who had been working on a nearby rooftop when the plane crashed. "The plane burst into bits like it was paper held together by thread. The impact just tore it apart."

The impact killed everyone on board and ignited the plane's 20,000 gallons of jet fuel. The WTC, proud symbol of American opportunity, turned into an inferno. Temperatures reached more than 2,000 degrees Fahrenheit (1,093 Celsius). The building's structural steel columns began to melt like plastic.

Woodward later would tell the story of his phone call to agents with the Federal Bureau of Investigation (FBI). His story was one piece in the puzzle of why a perfect September morning turned into a day of terror.

American Airlines Flight 11

United Airlines Flight 175

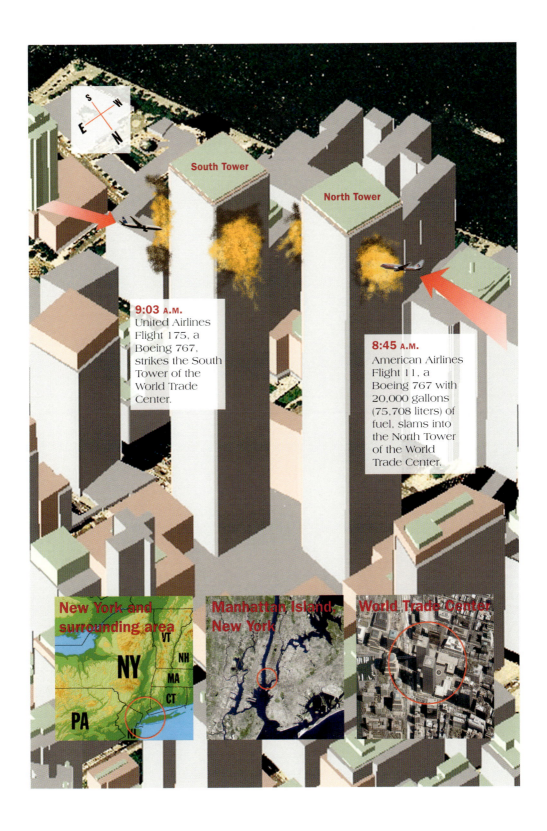

South Tower

North Tower

9:03 A.M.
United Airlines Flight 175, a Boeing 767, strikes the South Tower of the World Trade Center.

8:45 A.M.
American Airlines Flight 11, a Boeing 767 with 20,000 gallons (75,708 liters) of fuel, slams into the North Tower of the World Trade Center.

New York and surrounding area

VT
NH
NY
MA
CT
PA
NJ

Manhattan Island, New York

World Trade Center

Flying Bomb

United Airlines Flight 175 moments before crashing into the South Tower of the World Trade Center.

The Unthinkable Happens

THE TWIN TOWERS OF THE WTC WERE THE tallest buildings in the world when they were completed in the early 1970s. Many people regarded the towers as symbols of American wealth and success. Some 45,000 people worked in the towers, many of them in the financial industry. Another 150,000 people visited the towers each day.

When Flight 11 struck the North Tower on September 11, those inside felt a massive shudder. "The building was swaying, shaking, rocking," recounted one survivor. He had been on the 87th floor of the North Tower when the airplane struck it. He and others inside saw flying glass and papers outside their windows. Then thick clouds of smoke and fumes began to fill their offices. Almost immediately, the people in the tower headed for the dark, silent stairwells to make their way down to the ground floor. Many survivors recounted that people went down the many flights of stairs calmly.

The situation was different on floors above where the plane had struck. The smoke, heat, and flames were worse there. Many people panicked. Some broke windows to escape the flames and smoke. Explosions thrust some people out of the windows. Others fell or jumped to their deaths to avoid the flames.

Throughout Manhattan, people in the streets and in other buildings watched in horror. Just after 9 A.M. they saw something even worse. Yet another Boeing 767 smashed into the South Tower at about the 70th story. The jet hit the tower at an angle, slicing through the southeast corner. It was United Airlines Flight 175, diverted from Boston on its way to Los Angeles. All 65 people on board died instantly. "It was the most horrific scene I've ever seen," said New York Mayor Rudolph Giuliani, who witnessed the crash.

At 9:17 A.M., the Federal Aviation Administration (FAA) shut down all three airports that service New York City. Minutes later, the Port Authority of New York and New Jersey closed all bridges and tunnels to the New York City area. At 9:30 A.M., U.S. President George W. Bush announced that the nation had suffered a terrorist attack.

Ten minutes later, the FAA grounded all flight operations at U.S. airports. It was the first time that ever had been done. Yet it was too late. At 9:43 A.M., American Airlines Flight 77, with 64 people on board, crashed into the Pentagon near Washington, D.C. That flight had been diverted after taking off from Washington's Dulles Airport on its way to Los Angeles. The plane crashed into a heliport near the southwest side of the Pentagon, then cartwheeled into the building.

The impact sent a fireball of debris flying into the lower floors of the five-story steel and reinforced concrete building. Like the other flights, the plane banked just before impact. That ensured that the explosive fuselage would rip through as many floors as possible.

"At work, we had watched the attacks on the World Trade Center before we were hit," said a naval officer who survived the attack. "People in the office were commenting, 'If that can happen there, what's to stop it from happening here? ...No more than 10 minutes later it happened to us."

The Pentagon Attack

American Airlines Flight 77 slammed into the Pentagon in Washington, D.C., causing a section of the huge military building to collapse.

With part of the Pentagon in flames, officials quickly evacuated the White House. They then evacuated Congress and several other critical federal buildings.

Meanwhile in New York, the WTC continued to burn. The searing heat ravaged the steel structures. At 9:59 A.M., the South Tower collapsed. At 10:28 A.M., the North Tower also collapsed. Floor pancaked into floor as the structures dissolved, pushing out columns of choking smoke and flames. The twin towers had taken seven years to build. They took just seconds to collapse.

The force of the collapse equaled an earthquake measuring more than 2.0 on the Richter scale. Steel, glass, and concrete showered nearby streets and buildings. The dust and smoke turned the bright New York morning as dark as night. One eyewitness said simply, "All I could think was, 'This is not possible.' "

Across the nation, Americans watched and listened in horror. Televisions, radios, and the Internet delivered continuous coverage of the unthinkable events taking place. When people wondered if it could get any worse, news broke of yet another plane crash. United Flight 93 had crashed in rural Pennsylvania, just two miles from an elementary school. Officials thought that plane also had been hijacked. They guessed its target had been the White House, the U.S. Capitol, or Camp David.

Fortunately, Flight 93 never reached a target on the ground. Yet the 45 people on board now were dead in the smoking crater the crash left behind.

The Collapse

The South Tower of the World Trade Center crashes to the ground, killing thousands of people.

Pain and Grief

A firefighter pauses during the rescue effort. Hundreds of police and firefighters lost their lives on September 11.

In The Line Of Duty

AS WITH THE NORTH TOWER, SURVIVORS IN the South Tower raced to leave the building after it was struck. As they left the burning buildings, they saw firefighters and rescue workers running inside. "I know that the rescue people who were helping us didn't get out of the building," said one survivor.

The people of New York refer to their police officers as the finest. They call their firefighters the bravest. Never was that as true as on September 11. As flames and smoke took over the WTC, firefighters and police officers charged inside. They helped office workers to safety, lent oxygen masks to gasping people, and helped flush the soot out of victims' eyes. The rescuers climbed flight after flight of stairs in their heavy uniforms, loaded down with equipment. They worked feverishly to put out the flames in the towers. They used their axes to chop through walls and debris so people could escape. Others helped evacuate people from the other buildings in the WTC complex. Those buildings, now damaged by debris, also were in danger of collapsing.

Many firefighters still were rushing into the buildings even as they collapsed. "The toughest part was watching the firemen go back in the building as it was coming down," recalled one survivor. Added another, "They're a different breed. You've been taught to run out of a burning building. They're taught to run in." One bystander heard firefighters talk about entering the remaining 10 stories of the North Tower even after it had collapsed.

One firefighter ducked under his truck to escape the rain of debris from the falling towers. When he crawled back out, he found that everyone else in his squad was dead. Witnesses reported seeing many emergency vehicles heading toward the towers, but none came back.

More than 85 police officers are believed to have been killed in the line of duty that day. The New York Fire Department lost some 350 members. Among them were Fire Department Chief Peter Ganci, First Deputy Fire Commissioner William Feehan, Chief of Special Operations Ray Downey, and the department's chaplain, Father Mychal Judge. Father Judge was killed by falling debris while administering last rites to a dying firefighter. Ganci was killed when the North Tower collapsed. Ironically, in 1995, Downey had led a group of New York firefighters to Oklahoma City, Oklahoma, to help in the aftermath of that terrorist bombing.

Emergency medical workers also reported to the scene as soon as they learned of the disaster. Medical personnel from nearby hospitals quickly joined them. These workers had no operating rooms or examination rooms. They worked with what supplies they could carry. They tended to victims amidst knee-deep debris and choking smoke.

There were so many injured people the teams had to do triage. Triage means prioritizing medical conditions. Rescue workers did their work with the most seriously injured first. Those who were not as badly injured had to wait for help. Some paramedics worked 36-hour shifts.

Local hospitals quickly mobilized to treat survivors. St. Vincent's Hospital was closest to the scene. By 9 p.m., the St. Vincent's staff had treated more than 300 people. By 10 p.m., there were more medical staff and volunteers than there were patients. One doctor summed it up. "This is a nightmare," he said. "We haven't seen any wounded. You're either going to walk out of there or you're dead."

Rescue workers combed through the rubble of the towers and the Pentagon for days. Everyone hoped they might find survivors. Police and firefighters worked virtually non-stop through the night and into the next day. Many refused to stop to rest or to think about the horrors they were seeing. They found very few bodies while picking through the debris. Instead, they found many body parts.

Mayor Giuliani remembered the brave rescuers who gave their lives. He spoke at the funeral ceremonies for the fire department officials on the Saturday following the attacks. "They are heroes," he said. "They are like the heroes we had at Pearl Harbor. Each one of them was trying to save lives." Authorities estimate that had the firefighters, police officers, and rescue workers not helped evacuate people, the casualties in New York would have topped 20,000.

Firefighter Mike Kehoe assists in the evacuation effort in a stairwell of the North Tower. Kehoe escaped before the tower collapsed.

The Mayor Takes Charge

New York Mayor Rudolph Giuliani pulls off a dust mask while visiting the site in lower Manhattan where the twin towers of the World Trade Center were destroyed.

Taking Charge

RUDOLPH GIULIANI WAS ELECTED MAYOR OF New York City in 1993. Under his watch, New York City had enjoyed a reduction in crime, cleaner streets, and a new sense of order. At the same time, some people criticized him. They said he let problems in his marriage and his battle with cancer get in the way of his job.

On September 11, Giuliani was at the WTC within minutes of the crashes. For the next 36 hours, he worked non-stop mobilizing the city. Any complaints people might have had about him quickly disappeared. Though scheduled to leave office in January, 2002, due to term limits, some people wanted him to continue as a public servant.

President George W. Bush was visiting an elementary school in Florida when he learned of the attacks. For the first 10 hours, he was shuttled around the country due to security concerns. Finally, he demanded to return to Washington, D.C. Much to the surprise of his critics, he quickly took control.

In the days following September 11, President Bush mourned victims and comforted survivors. He rallied a devastated nation and began making plans for justice. He spoke out against violence against Arab Americans. He even scolded some conservative Christian leaders who said the U.S. deserved to be attacked because it was too liberal.

Working at his side were U.S. Secretary of Defense Donald Rumsfeld and U.S. Secretary of State Colin Powell. Both men are members of President Bush's Cabinet.

Rumsfeld advises President Bush on matters relating to the United States Armed Forces. He has an office at the Pentagon, and he was there when it was attacked. He immediately began helping injured people to safety. He wouldn't stop until he was pulled away to do his job. That job became planning a strategy for the U.S. to fight terrorism at home and abroad. He had to help determine what military actions that might involve. Then he had to identify which Armed Forces would carry out the required missions.

As Secretary of State, Colin Powell advises President Bush on matters relating to foreign countries. After the attacks, he cut short a visit to Latin America. Now he had a new and different mission. He had to get other nations around the world to support the U.S. in its war against terrorism. Sometimes that was easy. The United States has long-standing alliances with many nations. At other times, it was a difficult job. Powell had to contact leaders of some nations who once had considered the U.S. an enemy.

Powell had help in this task from British Prime Minister Tony Blair. Blair even earned the nickname "the persuader" for his work. He helped forge a coalition of nations to help the U.S. fight terrorism.

The attack on America also spurred a new interest in peace in the Middle East. Shortly after September 11, Palestinian leader Yassir Arafat called for a cease-fire with Israel. The two nations returned to the negotiating table. Many people hope it is the first step in ending that lengthy conflict.

A Determined President

President George W. Bush holds up the police shield of New York Police Officer George Howard, who died trying to save others in the World Trade Center.

31

Shock and Horror

Two women watch in horror as the World Trade Center towers collapse.

The Story Unfolds

THROUGHOUT THE DAY ON SEPTEMBER 11, news cameras swept the now-altered New York skyline and the burning Pentagon. America had a bird's-eye view of the destruction caused by three of the day's four hijacked planes. Yet the question remained—what about the fourth plane?

As the days went on, new information surfaced about Flight 93. The Boeing 757 had left Newark, New Jersey, at 8:01 A.M. It was headed to San Francisco, California. There were 38 passengers and seven crewmembers on board. At 10:37 A.M., it crashed 80 miles (129 km) southeast of Pittsburgh, Pennsylvania. The plane was going full speed at the time of impact. The largest piece remaining after the crash was a mere five feet (1.5 m) long.

Gradually, investigators pieced together what must have happened. A few relatives of the doomed passengers helped them. Some of them had received phone calls from their loved ones just before the plane crashed. "I know we're all going to die," passenger Tom Burnett told his wife over the phone. "There's three of us who are going to do something about it, if this plane is going down." His wife then told him about the attacks in New York and Washington. "I'm not giving up," he said.

Lyzbeth Glick also received a call from her husband, Jeremy. He told her the male passengers on the plane had voted to attack the hijackers. An air-phone supervisor also spoke with passenger Todd Beamer. Beamer said he and several others were going to jump a hijacker who claimed to have a bomb strapped to his body.

Investigators guess that these passengers, along with passenger Mark Bingham, decided to bring the plane down. They think the men wanted to avoid crashing into a building and killing more people. No one knows for certain what happened. However, these brave men quickly became heroes in the eyes of a grieving nation.

They were not alone. In New York and Washington, hundreds of ordinary people showed the bravery of heroes. At the World Trade Center, office workers helped a pregnant woman down the stairs to safety. Two others carried a woman in a wheelchair down 68 flights of stairs to escape. At the Pentagon, a group of Army officers were fleeing the building when they came upon a partially handicapped janitor. Without thinking, they picked him up and carried him to safety. Another soldier found a secretary virtually paralyzed by shock. He picked her up and carried her to safety as well.

Flight 93

Flowers, photographs, and mementos cover a makeshift memorial at the crash site of United Airlines Flight 93, near Shanksville, Pennsylvania.

In the streets of New York City, hundreds of strangers helped one another flee the billowing cloud of soot that turned the day into night. Two men heard cries and found a Brazilian tourist couple buried under the rubble. They uncovered them so they could get medical care.

Off-duty police officers, firefighters, and medical personnel rushed to the scene to help. Firefighters from throughout New England hurried to New York to relieve their exhausted counterparts. Volunteers formed bucket brigades to help remove debris in the search for survivors. Even a group of construction workers used their plywood to make gurneys for transporting injured people.

Outside New York and Washington, D.C., thousands of people donated blood. "Within two hours we had a line of donors that stretched out the front door," said a woman with the Red Cross in Portland, Oregon. The manager of a restaurant at Enron Field (home of the Astros) in Houston, Texas, baked 300 cookies to give to people giving blood. A medical team from Texas even drove more than 1,300 miles (2,092 km) to bring skin transplant material to aid burn victims.

A rescue dog searches for survivors in the rubble of the World Trade Center.

Not all of the heroes were human, however. Blind businessman Michael Hingson made it down 78 flights of stairs in the WTC thanks to his guide dog, Roselle. "Roselle was a hero for helping me to safety," he said. "But there were a lot of heroes out there. Everyone helped each other–down the stairwell, on the street–and everyone stuck together. We're all alive because of that. Everyone did what had to be done, and things were amazingly orderly."

Blood Drive

A donor gives much-needed blood at a Red Cross station the day after the terrorist attacks.

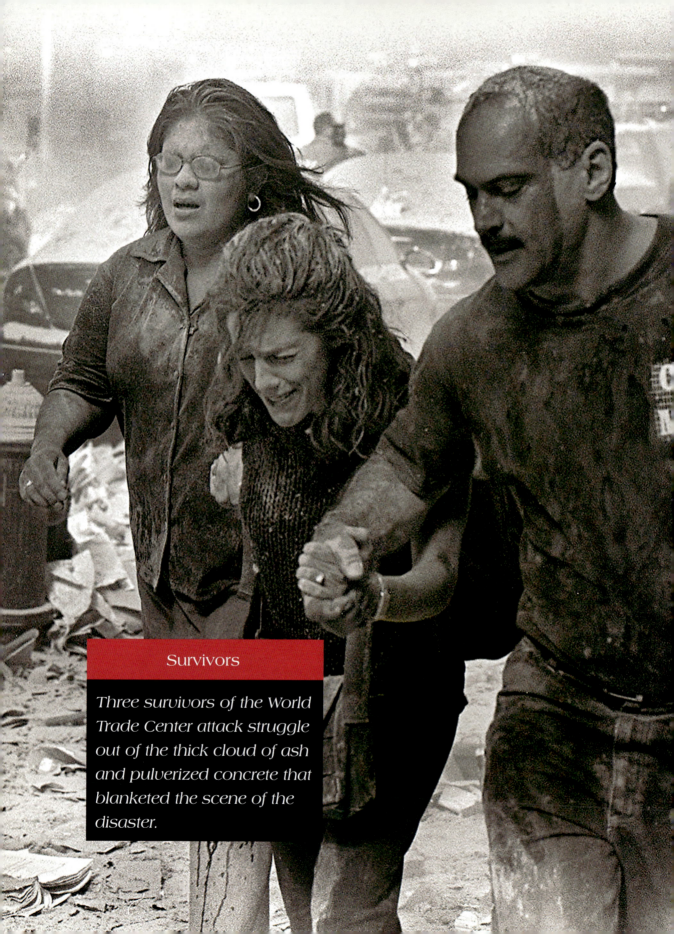

Survivors

Three survivors of the World Trade Center attack struggle out of the thick cloud of ash and pulverized concrete that blanketed the scene of the disaster.

Unspeakable Losses

WHEN THEY REACHED THE GROUND level, those fleeing the World Trade Center faced a rain of soot and ash so thick it was difficult to breathe. Many people had been injured by flames or broken glass. They wandered the streets in torn clothes, some badly burned, virtually all covered in ash and bleeding, until rescue workers could get them to a hospital. Hundreds of people were treated for smoke inhalation. Those people, however, were the lucky ones. They lived to tell their stories. Thousands of others were not so lucky.

All 265 passengers and crew on the four hijacked flights died that day. The death toll included executives, business people, retirees, and tourists. Some were famous, such as David Angell, creator and executive producer of the TV show *Frasier*, and CNN commentator Barbara Olson. Others were powerful, like Daniel Lewin, co-founder of Akamai Technologies, or Garnet "Ace" Bailey, a scout for the Los Angeles Kings hockey team.

A satellite view of Ground Zero.

There were young people, such as 11-year-old Bernard Brown, one of three elementary students going on an educational trip. There were old people, including 82-year-old Robert Norton, a retiree traveling with his wife. There were people from Germany, Australia, Israel, Ireland, and Switzerland. There was a priest who had survived World War II and a retired Navy admiral. There was a food pantry worker and a cameraman, along with lawyers, teachers, and doctors.

At the Pentagon, 126 are believed to have died, including a three-star Army general. Those suspected dead include 74 Army personnel, including 47 Army civilians and six contractors. Another 10 civilians working for Defense Department agencies also are missing and presumed dead. The Navy estimates it lost 33 active duty personnel, along with five civilians and four contractors.

At the WTC, the dead included hundreds of firefighters and police officers, as well as office workers, executives, and laborers. Death made no distinctions. Lawyers and investment bankers died alongside mail carriers and bus boys. Among the hardest hit was the bond brokerage firm of Cantor Fitzgerald. The firm's offices were at the site of impact with Flight 11.

Weeks after the attack, more than 6,000 Americans remained missing. In addition, officials in Great Britain estimate more than

100 British citizens lost their lives in the attacks. The nation of Japan also had been hit hard. The WTC housed offices for some 20 Japanese firms, including many of the country's largest banks.

The death toll was staggering. Even more staggering was the number of family members, friends, and relatives whose lives changed forever that day. Suddenly, there were thousands of new widows and widowers. In a flash, there were thousands of children with no mother, or no father. In one New York Fire Department unit alone, the attacks claimed the lives of 15 firefighters. Those 15 left behind 40 children who would never see their fathers alive again.

More people died on September 11, 2001, than had died in the surprise attack on Pearl Harbor in December 1941. That attack, which pushed the U.S. into World War II, killed some 2,400 people. The September 11 attacks also pushed the U.S. into a war. However, it would be a far different war than anything faced before. This enemy had no border, no army, and no government. The only thing that mobilized it was hatred.

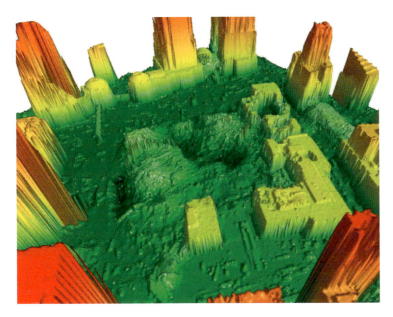

A 3-D positioning model of the WTC ruins and the surrounding area. The 3-D model helps locate original support structures, stairwells, elevator shafts, and basements.

41

Allies

A mourner weeps as she holds up an American flag outside Buckingham Palace in London, England, September 13, 2001. Queen Elizabeth ordered the U.S. national anthem to be played during the changing of the guard to honor victims of the September 11 terrorist attacks.

A World Mourns

I F THERE WAS ANY KIND OF SOLACE FOR AMERICANS following the attacks, it was that America was not grieving alone. The world was grieving with the United States.

As word of the attacks spread around the globe, hundreds of leaders in other nations called to voice their sorrow–and support. "We express deep shock at what we have witnessed in New York and Washington," said Lebanese Prime Minister Rafik Hariri. "...These tragic actions contradict all human and religious values."

"We are completely shocked," added Palestinian leader Yassir Arafat. "We completely condemn this very dangerous attack, and I convey my condolences to the American people...not only in my name but on behalf of the Palestinian people." Arafat's longtime rival, Israeli Prime Minister Ariel Sharon, gave his condolences as well. "The fight against terrorism is an international struggle of the free world against the forces of darkness."

"This is not a battle between the United States of America and terrorism but between the free world and democratic world and terrorism," said British Prime Minister Tony Blair. "We here in Britain stand shoulder to shoulder with our American friends in this hour of tragedy."

43

Around the world, there were spontaneous memorials and moments of silence. The 15-state European Union declared Friday, September 14, a day of mourning. Russia and the North Atlantic Treaty Organization (NATO) even issued a joint statement. Their statement said they would join forces to find out who was responsible for the attacks so justice could be done. Russia and the NATO nations used to be bitter adversaries. Even former U.S. adversaries such as Syria, Cuba, and Libya expressed their sadness over the attack.

Pope John Paul II publicly criticized the attacks and sent a telegram of condolence to President Bush. The government of Pakistan offered its support and assistance as well. Pakistan is a neighbor to Afghanistan, where many terrorists are believed to live and train.

Prayers for Peace

Pope John Paul II kneels in prayer for the victims of the terrorist attacks in America.

Clinging to Hope

Rescue workers dig around the clock in the desperate hope that somebody might still be alive, trapped under the rubble.

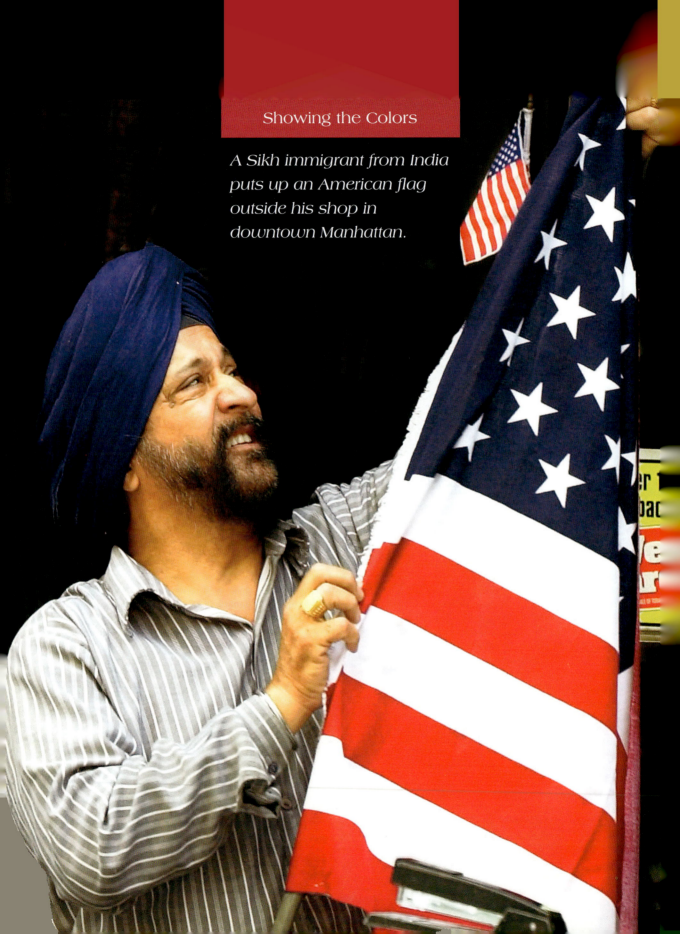

Showing the Colors

A Sikh immigrant from India puts up an American flag outside his shop in downtown Manhattan.

Pitching In

AMERICANS ARE KNOWN FOR RALLYING together in times of crisis. Around the nation, lines to donate blood formed within hours of the attacks. Almost immediately, Americans searched for ways to donate time or money to help in the rescue efforts and assist victims and their families.

Some hurried out to buy and display flags. Retail giant Wal-Mart reported it sold 116,000 flags on September 11 alone. Some people set up memorials in their communities to honor the dead. Americans held prayer vigils and memorial ceremonies. They wrote checks and collected pennies to donate. Strains of "God Bless America" and "America The Beautiful" filled churches, mosques, and synagogues.

In New York and Washington, D.C., hundreds of businesses donated their services. Wall Street's Regent Hotel converted its elegant ballroom into an around-the-clock relief center. Thanks to the help of a location manager for a television series, the hotel found a power generator so it could serve hot meals to police and rescue workers. Hotel staff even brought meals to the rubble pile that was once the WTC. They also set up cots so rescue workers could catch a quick nap.

Local restaurants donated food, as did New York's City Harvest charity. Businesses outside the attack area offered temporary employment to displaced workers who needed a job. Corporations donated much-needed money, food, medicine, and supplies. An organization in Oklahoma City even sent a shipment of teddy bears to help comfort elementary school children in New York and Washington, D.C.

Even the American Society for the Prevention of Cruelty to Animals (ASPCA) pitched in. ASPCA volunteers gathered donations of dog booties for the dogs working with the rescue workers to sniff out survivors. The dogs' feet had been getting cut by shards of glass and metal. With booties, they could do their jobs with less chance of injury. At the WTC site, people even held up hand-written signs cheering on rescue workers.

Americans also showed their respect for the dead. Many places of amusement such as Disneyland closed following the attacks. They remained closed out of respect. Professional sporting events were cancelled or delayed. Singer Madonna cancelled a concert performance. Organizers postponed both the Emmy Awards and the Latin Grammy Awards. Trading on the stock market halted for four days.

On the Friday following the attack, millions of Americans observed three minutes of silence. Even the Los Angeles Police Department reported a drop in crime following the attacks. Deputies in Los Angeles said some of the city's meanest streets were no longer filled with gangs. Instead, there were crowds of people holding candles and waving American flags.

On Friday, September 21, Hollywood showed its support as well. The *America: A Tribute to Heroes* telethon aired for two hours on more than 20 networks. The star-studded event raised more than $150 million for the United Way's September 11 Fund. All of the celebrities involved donated their time and talents.

American Heroes

A New York City firefighter surveys the wreckage of the World Trade Center.

Anger Boils Over

A Palestinian protester shows his hatred of Israel and the United States.

The Roots Of Hatred

A S INVESTIGATORS PIECED TOGETHER THE events of September 11, they uncovered a plot that shocked America. They painted a picture of a strong, unyielding hatred that few people could understand.

The facts slowly were revealed. Nineteen men hijacked the four airplanes using knife-like instruments, including box cutters and razor blades. The hijackers also claimed to have bombs strapped to their bodies. Further investigation revealed that some of the hijackers had been trained to fly jet airplanes. This meant they likely were the ones who piloted the planes into the buildings. They hailed from Egypt, Saudi Arabia, and the United Arab Emirates.

The U.S. Central Intelligence Agency (CIA) believes the hijackers were working for known terrorist network al-Qaeda (all-KIGH-dah). A soft-spoken man named Osama bin Laden (oh-SAH-ma bin LA-dun) started al-Qaeda, which means "the base." Bin Laden was born in 1957 into a wealthy Saudi Arabian family. He earned a civil engineering degree, and then left Saudi Arabia in 1979 to help the Afghan resistance fight the Soviet Union. Bin Laden started al-Qaeda to help with the Afghan resistance effort.

In 1990, Iraq invaded Kuwait and the U.S. launched Operation Desert Storm. Desert Storm helped push the Iraqi invaders out of Kuwait. Following Desert Storm, the U.S. left soldiers in Saudi Arabia to help prevent future skirmishes. Saudi Arabia also is a source of much of the oil upon which the U.S. depends.

Osama bin Laden was very upset about having U.S. soldiers in Saudi Arabia. The nation is considered home of the two most holy places in the religion of Islam (IS-lahm). He also hated the support the U.S. provided to Israel. He began to talk with other people about driving these infidels out of the holy lands. As time went on, it appeared his hatred of America grew. He declared a holy war against the U.S. He began recruiting more people to help him. The weapons in his holy war were acts of terrorism.

Target: Bin Laden

A photo of Osama bin Laden taken sometime in 1998.

Osama bin Laden is believed to have been behind many acts of terrorism. These include the bombing of two U.S. embassies in Africa in 1998 and the bombing of the USS *Cole* guided missile destroyer in 2000. Investigators also believe he was involved with the February 1993 bombing of the World Trade Center.

After the attacks, many people were quick to blame Arabic people for the deaths. However, many regions around the world have had to face terrorism. Terrorist acts can happen wherever people strongly disagree. For example, terrorist bombings have rocked Northern Ireland for years because of fighting between Catholics and Protestants.

The religion of Islam itself is not to blame, either. There is nothing in the Koran or in mainstream Islamic teaching that supports killing innocent people. In fact, the majority of the world's 1.2 billion Muslims (MOO-slims) do not support bin Laden's holy war. Rather, the events of September 11 are believed to be the result of a small group of extremists.

Shortly after the attacks, reports surfaced of verbal and physical attacks on innocent Muslims and people of Arabic heritage. Students tore down a Palestinian flag from a high school in Pennsylvania. Several Muslim students in the San Francisco area were taunted. A masked gunman opened fire on an Arabic gas station owner in Indiana. President Bush quickly asked the nation to avoid lashing out at people simply because of their ethnic background or religion. Other leaders reminded people that many Muslims had died in the attacks as well. Despite these pleas, many Arab Americans were frightened. "Now people are going to think that if you're Arabic, you're a terrorist," said one Arab woman.

A Grim Task

Firefighters slowly pick their way through the tangled, ghostly remains of the World Trade Center.

Picking Up The Pieces

THE TWO BILLION POUNDS (907,185 METRIC tons) of steel, glass, and concrete that once made up the second-tallest towers in the United States became a nine-story pile of rubble on September 11. The attacks and fires also left the streets of lower Manhattan covered with 10,000 tons (4.5 metric tons) of ash and soot. At first, rescuers clawed through the rubble by hand seeking survivors. They fought choking smoke and dust and smoldering debris. One rescuer said the rubble was still so hot he had to keep moving or his boots would start to melt. He and others worked through the night with the aid of giant searchlights. As time passed, the mission changed from rescue to clean-up.

The process was slow and dangerous. It was much like a game of pick-up sticks. Workers had to be careful that whatever they removed didn't trigger another avalanche of debris. They filled dump trucks at the rate of 12 trucks an hour. The rubble went to a nearby landfill where FBI agents searched through it for clues. Local pipe fitters and welders left their jobs to volunteer. They worked 12-hour shifts to help dismantle the ruins. Meanwhile, the papers, invoices, and files of some 45,000 workers blew around Manhattan. Some landed miles away.

Rescuers pulled five people from the WTC rubble. One woman was alive after having been trapped for 26 hours. The tiny number of survivors contrasted with the huge number of people still missing. Light poles around the disaster were plastered with flyers showing photos of people still missing.

As rescue workers trudged out of the area for rest or food, they faced hundreds of anxious friends and relatives. The people would wave pictures at them asking, "Have you seen her? Have you seen him?"

Even as people searched for missing family and friends, officials put plans into action to help victims pick up their own pieces. Several federal agencies announced they would make money available to help victims pay for counseling, medical bills,

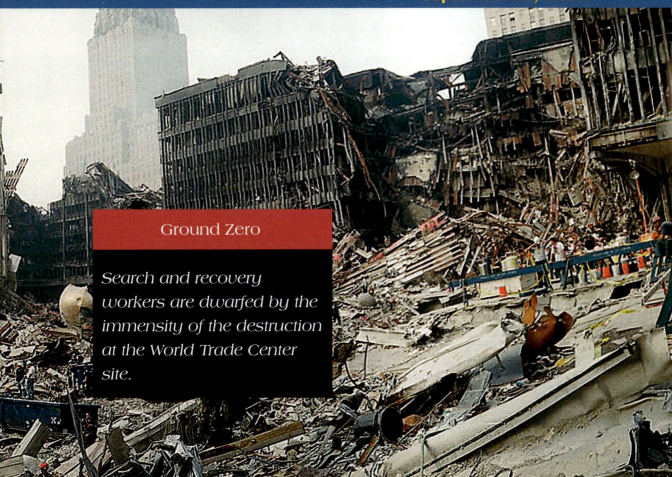

Ground Zero

Search and recovery workers are dwarfed by the immensity of the destruction at the World Trade Center site.

and lost wages. New York Governor George Pataki announced plans to provide a free college education for family members of WTC victims, including emergency personnel.

Beyond the WTC itself, New York City officials worked to assess other buildings damaged by the attacks. In addition to the twin towers, the attacks destroyed a nearby hotel and two smaller buildings in the WTC complex. Other nearby buildings had partially collapsed or were damaged enough to make them unstable.

In Washington, D.C., workers continued to clear out rubble from the damaged Pentagon. In the rest of the fortress-like building, it soon became more than business as usual. It became the center of a new war against terrorism.

Operation Enduring Freedom

O N SEPTEMBER 11, PRESIDENT GEORGE W. Bush declared war on terrorism. He warned Americans that such a war would be neither quick nor painless. He also warned the rest of the world that they would have to make a decision. "Either you are with us or with the terrorists," he said. "From this day forward, any nation that continues to harbor or support terrorism will be regarded by the United States as a hostile regime."

President Bush and other leaders discussed military options. One involved sending soldiers to Afghanistan, where many terrorists are suspected to live. Another option would be to send soldiers to other nations suspected of harboring terrorists.

Two weeks after the attacks, Secretary of Defense Donald Rumsfeld announced that this new U.S. anti-terrorism campaign would be called Operation Enduring Freedom. He added that it would be different from any other war in history. "This is about self-defense," he said. "The only way we can defend against terrorism is by taking the fight to the terrorists."

One of the first tasks of Enduring Freedom is to find Osama bin Laden, who is suspected to be in Afghanistan. As of 2001, Afghanistan was controlled by the Taliban, whose leaders are sympathetic to bin Laden and his holy war against the U.S.

At home, President Bush worked quickly to prevent further terrorist attacks. Security measures at airports were increased dramatically. Military forces were put on alert. Bush even announced the creation of a new cabinet-level position. Pennsylvania Governor Tom Ridge was appointed to the new position of director of the Office of Homeland Security.

"Great harm has been done to us," Bush told the public during a presidential address September 13. "We have suffered great loss. And in our grief and anger, we have found our mission and our moment."

America Strikes Back

A U.S. Navy F/A-18C Hornet lands on the flight deck of the aircraft carrier U.S.S. Carl Vinson *during Operation Enduring Freedom.*

You Can Make A Difference

JUST ONE WEEK AFTER THE ATTACKS, PRESIDENT Bush announced a new web site had been created to make it easier for people to help. The web site features links to organizations helping victims and survivors to put their lives back together. The **American Liberty Partnership** can be accessed at the following web site: www.libertyunites.org

Additionally, a number of national organizations providing relief, development, and refugee assistance can use your help. Following are names and contact information.

The September 11th Fund

The United Way of New York and the New York Community Trust have set up a special fund to help attack victims and their families. You can donate money to help emergency assistance agencies do their job. Send donations in care of United Way, 2 Park Avenue, New York, New York, 10016. Or, call (212) 251-4035, or visit www.uwnyc.org.

The American Red Cross

You can help make a difference by donating money to the American Red Cross Disaster Relief Fund. To donate, call 1-800-HELP-NOW, or visit www.redcross.org.

New York Firefighter and Police Survivors Fund

Help the families left behind by the brave firefighters, police officers, and emergency medical personnel who died trying to save others. The International Association of Firefighters is collecting donations at two organizations. You can send donations to the Widows and Children's Fund, NYFD–Uniformed Firefighters Association, 204 East 24th Street, New York, New York, 10010. Or, send contributions to the attention of Joe Mahoney at the Police Benevolent Association, Widows and Children's Fund, 40 Fulton Street, New York, New York, 10038.

Save the Children Fund

Lend a hand to the children of attack victims by calling the Save the Children Fund for Children in Crisis at (800) 728-3843. Or, visit www.savethechildren.org.

The Salvation Army

The Salvation Army also is accepting cash donations. These donations will go to the agency's Disaster Services Fund. To donate, call (800) SAL-ARMY.

If you can't donate money, you can still help prevent future acts of hatred and terrorism in your own community. Check out 101 Tools for Tolerance at www.tolerance.org for ideas of what you can do at home and in your school.

Timeline of Terror, 9-11-01

8:45 A.M.   American Airlines Flight 11 crashes into the North Tower of the World Trade Center, setting it on fire.

9:03 A.M.   United Airlines Flight 175 slams into the South Tower of the World Trade Center, setting it on fire as well.

9:30 A.M.   President George W. Bush announces that the nation has suffered a terrorist attack.

9:40 A.M.   The Federal Aviation Administration halts all flight operations at all U.S. airports.

9:43 A.M.   American Airlines Flight 77 crashes into the Pentagon.

10:05 A.M.   The South Tower of the World Trade Center collapses.

10:10 A.M.   A portion of the Pentagon collapses.

10:28 A.M.   The North Tower of the World Trade Center collapses.

10:48 A.M.   Police confirm the crash of United Flight 93 in Pennsylvania.

11:02 A.M.   New York Mayor Rudolph Giuliani asks New Yorkers to stay home and orders everyone south of Canal Street to leave the area.

1:04 P.M.   President Bush promises the U.S. will find and punish those people responsible for the attacks.

1:44 P.M.   Aircraft carriers USS *George Washington* and USS *John F. Kennedy* along with five other warships leave Norfolk, Virginia, for the New York coast to further protect the area.

4:00 P.M.   U.S. officials say they believe Osama bin Laden is connected to the attacks.

5:20 P.M.   The 47-story Building 7 of the World Trade Center collapses.

7:45 P.M.   New York officials report that nearly 80 police officers and up to 200 firefighters are believed to have been killed during rescue operations.

8:30 P.M.   President Bush addresses the nation.

Glossary

cabinet
The top advisers to the president.

extremists
People who resort to extreme measures.

fuselage
The central part of an airplane.

infidel
A person who is an unbeliever in respect to a particular religion such as Christianity or Islam.

Koran
The sacred texts of the religion of Islam.

mosque
A Muslim house of worship.

synagogue
A Jewish house of worship.

triage
A system used to determine who gets medical care first in an emergency.

Index